NEW LANCHESTER STRATEGY

SALES AND MARKETING STRATEGY FOR THE STRONG

Volume 3

NEW LANCHESTER STRATEGY

(The Comic Book)
SALES AND MARKETING STRATEGY FOR THE STRONG
Volume 3

by
Shinichi Yano

Ilustrated by Kenichi Sato
Translated by Connie Prener

Lanchester Press Incorporated
Sunnyvale, California
http://www.lanchester.com

The persons and organizations appearing in this book are fictitious and have no
relation to actual persons or organizations.

ISBN 1-57321-005-6.

Library of Congress Card Number: 96-77528

Editor: John Schuler
Translator: Connie Prener
Electronic imaging: Costas Schuler
Printed and bound by Patson's Press, Sunnyvale, California.
Lanchester Press Incorporated, P.O. Box 60621, Sunnyvale, CA 94086, U.S.A.
http://www.lanchester.com

Contents

A Note on the English Edition

This third volume of Shinichi Yano's *New Lanchester Strategy*, describes strategy and tactics for the well-established company. Careful reading of this book will give considerable insight into what goes on inside a Japanese company during thrust and counter-thrust for marketplace dominance.

Even more significant, particularly for readers in the West, is that the "myth" of the invincible samurai warrier is finally laid to rest. Much of the writings on the so-called Japanese marketing strategy have relied heavily on a mixture of homilies from Sun-Tzu, Musashi, and Mishima, mixed with a dash of Attila the Hun and Von Clausewitz.

In reality, the science of military technology has progressed somewhat since the days of the samurai warriers. A few well-aimed bursts from a machine gun will dispatch a fair-sized army of samurai warriors. The Japanese marketers are fully aware of the power of concentration articulated by F. W. Lanchester, who wrote on October 2, 1914; "with modern long-range weapons - fire arms, in brief; the concentration of superior numbers gives an immediate superiority in the combatant ranks, and the numerically inferior force finds itself under a far heavier fire, man for man, than it is able to return."

Widespread use of the "samurai warrior" model of marketing strategy, as promoted by innumerable books on the subject, is a stumbling block for Western readers. The "samurai warrior" model is essentially the one-on-one combat that takes place under conditions described by Lanchester's Linear Law of combat. Consequently, Western marketers are going into battle with, at best, half a theory and ignorant of the awesome power of concentration represented by Lanchester's Second, or N-Squared Law of Combat.

The realization that a more comprehensive theory of marketing strategy exists is what the late Thomas S. Kuhn would call a paradigm shift, more colloquially known as a whack on the side of the head.

John Schuler
Sunnyvale
July 1996

Message from Kenichi Sato, Cartoonist and Illustrator

To tell you the truth, when I was asked to produce Lanchester Strategy material in comic book form, I wasn't quite sure that I was up to the task. At the time, I knew almost nothing about the Lanchester Strategy. As I got better acquainted with the Lanchester Strategy, I became even more aware of the difficulties in translating it to the comic format. But, at the same time, I was inspired to create a product that anyone could understand. Dr. Yano helped me a great deal with my work, as did the editorial staff.

To my surprise, the process went smoothly, though I exerted an incredible amount of energy, due to the tight deadline. Human beings seem to manage to surpass their perceived capabilities when faced with a challenge like this one. Both Volumes I and II were very well received, which was a source of great pride to me. I have endeavoured to exploit the merits of the comic-book format to the best of my ability. It gives me pleasure that this format is particularly suited to how-to books, which are immensely popular now.

I am now preparing for my next project, a new series, *Applying the New Lanchester Strategy,* which will keep me very busy. I have grown fond of the characters in this first series, and it will be somewhat hard to say goodbye to them. Incidentally, I took the name Shinsaku Sakamoto (the protagonist) from the names of two nineteenth-century heroes, Ryoma Sakamoto and Shinsaku Takasugi. I enjoy speculating about what they would accomplish if both of them were alive today and were active in the corporate world.

Finally, I would like to thank Dr. Shinichi Yano for giving me the opportunity to work on this project, and the members of his staff for their invaluable assistance.

Kenichi Sato

Forward by the Author

This volume discusses strategies for the strong. Companies that are in a strong position should read it, of course, but so should their weaker rivals, so they'll know what sort of strategies the strong might be using. You need to be able to "read" your rivals. When the weak know how the strong are operating, they can develop powerful strategies.

By the strong, I mean market leaders, but there is more than one type of market leader. There are market leaders that are ahead of their nearest competitors by a factor of $\sqrt{3}$, and then there are others without such a huge lead. Number-one companies tend to concentrate on defense, but they may fail to sense an oncoming crisis. They may become overconfident, and rest on their laurels. Many of them want merely to stay on the safe side.

Someone once said that defense is three times as much work as offense, and he was correct. When a top-ranking company lets its guard down, its market share is bound to drop. Remember that defending your position is a matter of winning a succession of battles. You have to keep winning. Also, when a strong company, regardless of its strength, has not yet become number one, it must go on the offensive to capture that position.

This volume, like its predecessor, Volume 2, Strategy of the Weak, consists of six chapters.

Chapter 1 discusses the matching operation. This means following, or imitating your rival, and it is the strategy to use to counteract the differentiation strategy of the weak. The matching operation is an important strategy not only for the strong, but also for the weak to use against their lower-ranking rivals.

Chapter 2 discusses wide-area battles. When you wage a wide-area battle, you are competing in an arena without boundaries. This strategy is intended to offset the local-battle strategy used by the weak.

Chapter 3 discusses stochastic battles. In a stochastic battle, you force your enemies, or even your allies, to battle against each other. This is a strategy to use to counteract the single-combat strategy used by the weak.

Chapter 4 discusses remote battles. Remote battles are used against close combat, a strategy of the weak. They involve the following two strategies: (1) using wholesalers to the best possible advantage, and (2) bolstering advertising and publicity campaigns.

Chapter 5 discusses comprehensive battles. These battles take advantage of the comprehensive strength of the strong, and serve to counteract the one-point concentration strategy used by the weak.

Chapter 6 discusses inducement operations. This strategy is used against feint operations launched by the weak. It is a means of forestalling weaker rivals by preventing them from using the differentation or one-point concentration strategies.

This volume completes the three-volume Introduction to Lanchester Strategy. It features Shinsaku Sakamoto of Company W. It is the story of the battle between Company W and its rival, Company B. Manufacturers, retailers, and representatives of the service sector also appear in this drama.

I believe that in this volume, as in its predecessor, Volume 2, the expert hand of our cartoonist, Kenichi Sato, is even more in evidence than in the previous two volumes. We hope our readers will forgive any infelicities that may have arisen due to time constraints.

Each story is based on events that actually occurred, but because of the format, we have had to show rises in market share and reversals in a way that makes them seem less complicated than they actually were.

We are now planning to publish a series showing ways to apply the New Lanchester Strategy, which will cover regional strategy.

In closing, I would like to express my deepest gratitude to Mr. Matsumoto, president of the Wako Printing Company, as well as to the Messrs. Takahashi, Suganoya, and Mabuchi and the entire staff of Wako Printing Company, to Mr. Miura of the CUE Research Institute, to Editor-in-chief Homma and Mr. Sakuma of the Japan Management Consultants Association, and to the many others whose assistance has been invaluable.

August 1986
Shinichi Yano

CAST OF CHARACTERS

SHINSAKU SAKAMOTO

Supervisor, Section 3, Sales Department, Company W, and the hero of our story. He has doubts about traditional sales strategy, so instructs his team to employ the New Lanchester Strategy. The team engineers a reversal, unseating Company B from its top-ranking position, and Company W becomes number one. Sakamoto succeeds in implementing the New Lanchester Strategy at Company W.

YUJI KONDO

Supervisor, Section 3, Sales , Company W. Sakamoto's rival. Opposed to Lanchester Strategy, and tries to thwart Sakamoto.

SHINTARO SHIMADA

One of the most promising supervisors at Company B. Defeated by Sakamoto's team, Shimada launches a new offensive.

Sakamoto's Staff

| MORI | MATSUDA | YAMAGISHI | SUGIYAMA | MURAKAMI |

TAIZO MASUMURA

Director, Sales Department, Company W.
A no-nonsense, dedicated man who lives for his work. Originally skeptical about the Lanchester Strategy, but recognizes Sakamoto's successes, and implements the New Lanchester Strategy at Company W.

MOTOHARU OHASHI

Manager, Section 3, Sales. Interested in the Lanchester Strategy. Supports Sakamoto's efforts, though not openly.

RUMIKO KAWANO

A cheerful, lively office worker who is attracted to Sakamoto.

KATAYAMA

Sakamoto's college classmate and friend. Executive of a family restaurant owned by his father.

HAMADA

Katayama's friend. Runs a supermarket with his father-in-law.

KOIKE

In college ahead of Matsuda. Runs a wholesale food business started by his father.

ONO

President of industrial supply manufacturer. Goes to the same athletic club as Sakamoto.

CHAPTER ONE

MATCHING OPERATIONS

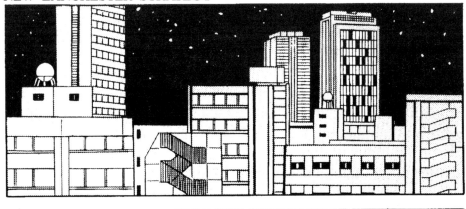

3

THA ... THAT'S EXACTLY WHAT HAPPENED. THEY LOWERED THEM BY 10%.

OH. THAT'S WHAT HAPPENED TO MATSUDA AT KOYAMA COMPANY, RIGHT?

THESE DAYS COMPANY B SEEMS TO BE OBSESSED WITH US.

NO, NO ... IF COMPANY B IS LOWERING ITS PRICES ACROSS THE BOARD, THEN WE'VE GOT TO DO SOMETHING ABOUT THAT.

I JUST DIDN'T TRY HARD ENOUGH.

MR. SAKAMOTO! COMPANY B IS ...

OH NO, NOT THEM AGAIN!

COMPANY B IS PRACTICALLY GIVING AWAY ITS MERCHANDISE!!

THEY'RE STEALING YOUR CLIENTS, TOO, SUGIYAMA?

THIS IS REALLY BAD.

AND JUST WHEN WE'D BEATEN THEM. IF THEY MAKE A COUNTER-ATTACK ...

5

MATSUDA, I'D LIKE YOU TO TAKE CHARGE OF TODAY'S MEETING.

YES, SIR.

I'D LIKE ALL OF YOU TO REPORT WHAT YOU'VE LEARNED ABOUT THE DISCOUNTS COMPANY B IS OFFERING.

IN MY TERRITORY, THEY'RE DISCOUNTING ALL THEIR PRODUCTS.

MINE, TOO. THEY'RE REALLY STUBBORN.

7

MINE, TOO, BUT I FOUND OUT THAT THERE'S A NEW MANAGER THERE.

THE STORY IS THAT THE FORMER MANAGER GOT SENT TO THE BOONDOCKS WHEN WE BEAT THEM OUT.

THE NEW MANAGER'S NAME IS SHIMADA. I HEAR HE'S REALLY SHARP.

AND THE RUMOR IS THAT SHIMADA'S BEEN STUDYING THE LANCHESTER STRATEGY.

WHAT??!!

8

MR. OHASHI TOLD ME THAT COMPANY B HAS TAKEN AN INTEREST IN THE LANCHESTER STRATEGY.

A FRIEND OF MINE SPOTTED HIM AT A LANCHESTER STRATEGY SEMINAR.

HOW MUCH ARE THEY USING IT?

OUR ONLY SOURCE IS THE INFORMATION YOU'VE COME UP WITH. MATSUDA, PLEASE CONTINUE.

WE KNOW THAT COMPANY B IS DISCOUNTING ALL ITS PRODUCTS IN ALL REGIONS. WHAT ELSE ARE THEY DOING?

I HEARD THEY'RE HELPING THEIR AGENCIES SET UP INFORMATION NETWORKS.

THEY'RE GOING TO SEND A MONTHLY NEWSLETTER TO THEIR USERS STARTING NEXT MONTH.

THAT MEANS COMPANY B IS DOING FULL-SCALE DIFFERENTIATION.

THAT'S PURE LANCHESTER STRATEGY.

IF THEY'VE GONE THAT FAR, THEN ...

IT'LL BE HARD FOR US TO FIGHT BACK.

CHIEF ...

DON'T WORRY. I HAVE AN IDEA. I'LL TELL YOU ABOUT IT AT TOMORROW'S MEETING.

THESE ARE HARD TIMES BOTH FOR US AND COMPANY B. LET'S NOT GET DISCOURAGED.

YES, SIR.

THAT'S WHAT I TOLD THEM, BUT ...

I DON'T HAVE ANY GOOD IDEAS THIS TIME.

SAKAMOTO.

RATTLE

OH, MR. MASUMURA, YOU'RE STILL HERE?

YES, I'VE BEEN REALLY BUSY. BY THE WAY, IT LOOKS LIKE THE ODA-NISHIJIMA TEAM IS ABOUT TO PULL A REVERSAL ON COMPANY B.

THE OTHER TEAMS ARE DOING WELL, TOO — EXCEPT FOR YOUR TEAM.

YES, AND RIGHT AFTER WE INTRODUCED THE LANCHESTER STRATEGY HERE. I'M SORRY.

BUT PLEASE WAIT AND SEE. AFTER ALL, WE STARTED USING IT BEFORE THEY DID.

12

13

15

AH, MR. OHASHI!

OH, IT'S YOU, SAKAMOTO. ON YOUR WAY HOME?

I STOPPED IN TO SEE A CLIENT IN THE AREA.

WHAT'S THE MATTER? I'VE NEVER SEEN YOU LOOKING LIKE THIS.

COMPANY B IS USING THE LANCHESTER STRATEGY.

GOOD FOR THEM! IF WE'RE USING THE SAME WEAPONS, WE'LL WIN, SINCE WE'RE THE STRONG ARMY. ISN'T THAT HOW IT WORKS?

YES, THAT'S RIGHT, BUT ...

SAKAMOTO, DON'T GIVE UP.

WELL, THIS IS MY STOP.

GOODNIGHT, THEN.

WITH THE SAME WEAPONS, THE STRONGER ARMY WINS ... THE SAME WEAPONS ....

HEY, I'VE GOT IT!

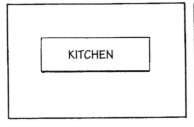

KITCHEN

UM-HM. HE'S BEEN IN A MEETING SINCE EARLY THIS MORNING.

AREN'T YOU WORRIED, RUMIKO?

HEY, RUMIKO, DID YOU HEAR ABOUT MR. SAKAMOTO'S PROBLEM?

NO, I HAVE FAITH IN HIM.

HE'LL COME UP WITH A GOOD PLAN, SO DON'T YOU WORRY.

SHE REALLY BELIEVES IN HIM!

I REALLY AM A LITTLE WORRIED, THOUGH ...

CLAP

18

CONFERENCE ROOM NO. 2

YOU KNOW THAT THE LANCHESTER STRATEGY INCLUDES STRATEGIES FOR BOTH THE STRONG AND THE WEAK, RIGHT?

WE'VE BEEN USING THE STRATEGY FOR THE WEAK.

BUT NOW THAT WE'RE NUMBER ONE, WE HAVE TO SHIFT TO THE STRATEGY FOR THE STRONG.

WHEN I HEARD THAT COMPANY B IS DOING DIFFERENTIATION, I THOUGHT WE SHOULD DO MORE OF THAT.

BUT WE DON'T. WE LEAD BOTH IN SALES AND MARKET SHARE. THAT'S DIFFERENTIATION RIGHT THERE.

WE NEED TO ADOPT THE BASIC STRATEGY FOR THE STRONG — A "MATCHING" OPERATION.

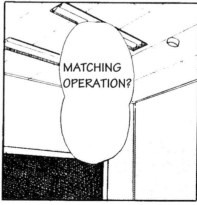

MATCHING OPERATION?

MATCHING OPERATIONS

21

22

HMM ...

ALSO, WE HAVE TO GET THE WORD OUT THAT WE'RE THE TOP MANUFACTURER.

MATCH COMPANY B	1. OFFER 10% DISCOUNTS 2. ASSIST AGENCIES IN SETTING UP AN INFORMATION NETWORK 3. DISTRIBUTE A MONTHLY NEWSLETTER TO USERS
ADVERTISE STRENGTH	1. IMPRESS UPON USERS THAT WE ARE THE TOP-RANKING MANUFACTURER AT EVERY POSSIBLE OPPORTUNITY
AGENCY STRATEGY	1. INSIST THAT AGENCY REPRESENTATIVES GO ALONG ON SALES CALLS 2. ASK DIRECTORS AND MANAGERS TO VISIT AGENCY EXECUTIVES

SO, LET'S FOLLOW THIS STRATEGY. FORTUNATELY, WE WERE ABLE TO GET INFORMATION ABOUT COMPANY B EARLY, SO WE'VE GOT TIME.

I'D LIKE TO GET APPROVAL FROM THE MANAGER AND THE DIRECTOR FOR THIS MATCHING OPERATION AGAINST COMPANY B.

LET'S START RIGHT AWAY BY EMPHASIZING OUR POSITION OF STRENGTH.

I MENTIONED THE STRATEGY TO USE ON OUR AGENCIES BECAUSE THE STRONG MUST BE ABLE TO MANIPULATE THEIR AGENCIES SKILL-FULLY.

YOU PROBABLY KNOW THAT OUR CUSTOMERS AND OUR INDUSTRY, AS WELL AS EVERYBODY IN THIS COMPANY, ARE WATCHING WHAT OUR TEAM DOES.

OUR CONDUCT WILL AFFECT THE ENTIRE SALES DIVISION. WE'RE ALREADY NUMBER ONE. NOW LET'S TRIPLE THE DISTANCE BETWEEN US AND COMPANY B.

24

REMEMBER, WE'RE THE STRONG ARMY. LET'S HAVE CONFIDENCE IN OURSELVES.

YES, SIR!

THE SAKAMOTO TEAM REGAINS ITS FIGHTING SPIRIT ...

AND BACKED UP BY THE MANAGER AND DIRECTOR, DEVOTES ALL ITS ENERGY TO THE OPERATION.

IT MONITORS COMPANY B'S MOVEMENTS. WHENEVER COMPANY B DOES A NEW TYPE OF DIFFERENTIATION, THE TEAM MATCHES IT.

25

SEVERAL MONTHS LATER...

WHEW!

COMPANY B IS REALLY SERIOUS THIS TIME!

WHAT KIND OF GUY IS THIS SHIMADA? HE JUST DOESN'T GIVE UP!

CHIEF, ARE YOU LISTENING? MY EFFORTS AT COMPANY K HAVE PAID OFF!

WHAT?!

COMPANY L SHOULD BE OURS VERY SOON.

26

ALL RIGHT! WE'RE ON A ROLL. LET'S HOPE IT LASTS.

SEVERAL DAYS LATER ...

CHIEF, WE DID IT!

....
........!! ....!!

WAIT, WAIT! ONE AT A TIME, PLEASE!

NOW, WHAT DID YOU DO?

OKAY, THEN I'LL START. YAMAMURA CO. USED TO FAVOR COMPANY B, BUT THEY'VE AGREED TO FEATURE OUR PRODUCTS.

I GOT AN ORDER FROM COMPANY Y!

IS THAT RIGHT? NICE WORK, BOTH OF YOU!

OUR MATCHING OPERATION WORKED!

CHIEF, I'LL KNOW TOMORROW ABOUT COMPANY Q, A MAJOR USER. THINGS ARE LOOKING GOOD FOR US.

SO YOU DID IT, MORI! GOOD JOB!

OKAY! WE'RE GOING TO BE NUMBER ONE IN A BIG WAY!

THAT'S ENOUGH FOR TODAY. LET'S GO OUT AND CELEBRATE.

HOORAY!!

WOW! LOOK WHO'S HERE.

THANKS FOR YOUR HARD WORK, SAKAMOTO TEAM! NOW WE'RE NUMBER ONE COMPANY-WIDE.

I STILL CAN'T BELIEVE IT.

WE OWE ALL OF THIS TO THE NEW LANCHESTER STRATEGY.

YUP.

MR. MASUMURA, MR. OHASHI! THANK YOU FOR YOUR SUPPORT.

NO PROBLEM. YOU CAN ASK ME ANYTIME.

THAT'S MY JOB, SAKAMOTO.

WE CAN'T RELAX YET, BUT WE HAVE ATTAINED THE GOAL WE SET. YOU'VE ALL PUT IN SO MANY HOURS.

YOUR WIVES AND GIRLFRIENDS MUST HAVE MISSED YOU.

THESE ARE SMALL TOKENS OF APPRECIATION FROM ME AND OHASHI.

GIVE THEM TO YOUR WIVES OR GIRLFRIENDS.

30

THE DIRECTOR REALLY HAS CLASS!

YES, HE DOES.

I DON'T HAVE A WIFE OR A GIRLFRIEND.

GIVE IT TO YOUR MOTHER OR YOUR SISTER, OR SAVE IT FOR THE FUTURE.

HA, HA, HA!

IT'S REALLY NOTHING SPECIAL.

MR. OHASHI, CAN'T YOU STAY A WHILE LONGER?

NO. BUT YOU GUYS HAVE A GOOD TIME!

31

I PROBABLY DON'T NEED TO SAY THIS, BUT COMPANY B ISN'T GOING TO TAKE THIS LYING DOWN.

THEY'LL ATTACK US AGAIN.

YES, I AGREE

WE'LL HAVE TO STAY ALERT.

I'VE LEARNED THAT DEFENDING A STRONG POSITION IS A REAL PAIN, THOUGH.

KEEP UP THE GOOD WORK, SAKAMOTO.

I'LL TRY.

I'M GOING NOW. EVERYONE'S WAITING FOR YOU.

HAVE FUN!

GOOD-NIGHT, THEN.

I'M STARVING. LET'S GO GET SOMETHING TO EAT.

SURE! GREAT IDEA!

SUMMARY

The strategy of the weak focuses on offensive moves, but the strategy of the strong stresses defense. Defending your position means keeping your rival from attacking you, i.e., preventing the weak from using the strategy of the weak.

The main strategy of the weak is differentiation (see Volume 2). Differentiation is a matter of raising the level of weapon performance and the skills of those who wield those weapons (raising E, according to the Lanchester Laws). When a weaker rival begins differentiating, a strong company needs only to match the rival's level of weapon performance and users' skill. Doing so negates the differentiation strategy used by the weak.

For instance, if a small (weak) army has guns, and a large (strong) army has only swords and spears, the battle that ensues is bound to be a desperate one. On the other hand, if the strong army also has guns, it is clearly at an advantage. This is called "matching." "Matching" means lowering the weak's E level to 1 and, in terms of sales strategy, it means matching the weaker rivals' differentiation.

The purpose of a matching operation is to obliterate the effects of any differentiation done by the weaker rival. It is also a psychological weapon, because it sends a message to the weak. It tells them that a strong army is not vulnerable to their attacks.

When the strong have matched the weak any number of times, the weak will eventually give up. However, matching operations are futile unless they are implemented expeditiously. If the strong delay in launching them, the weak have more time to use the differentiation process to their advantage. The strong must not allow the weak to gain confidence, since one of the reasons the weak are trying to win is to gain confidence and momentum.

Momentum, once gained, is difficult to curb. To do so, the strong must be constantly vigilant of the moves made by the weak, and be prepared to match every one of them. Also required is a system for acquiring as much information as possible about their rivals.

To strengthen this information-gathering system, you need to

1. Ensure that everyone involved is aware of the problem
2. Approach as many clients as possible
3. Set up a company-wide information network

Here are the types of matching operations that can be used to counter the weak's attempts to differentiate:

1. Matching product differentiation

When a weak manufacturer starts differentiating its products, the strong must put similar products on the market immediately. However, when time does not allow that, even a copycat product will do, as long as customers are not aware of any difference.Even if they are set up to get a new product on the market quickly, some manufacturers prefer to wait until demand for a new product has increased, and then use their prodigious selling power to take over the market.

2. Matching merchandise differentiation

Since the differentiation of merchandise for special purposes hinges on a company's planning ability and ingenuity, it is easy to match differentiation of this sort if your information-gathering capabilities are good. However, since differentiation of inventories in the retail or service sectors often varies with the day of the week, time of day, the weather, and other factors, you may lose your opportunity if you don't keep constant watch over prevailing circumstances.

3. Matching service differentiation

The service sector embraces a wide range of businesses. If the weak are making headway in this area, their efforts must be matched immediately. This is another area in which information-gathering is crucial, since many aspects of service are not easily defined, and customers' ratings will vary.

4. Matching publicity campaigns (direct mail, flyers)

When a weaker rival launches a publicity campaign, the strong should not only match it, but also counter the weaker rivals' campaign with sheer volume.

5. Matching channel differentiation

In today's changing world, it's difficult to know who is handling what products. This is an opportunity for the weak to differentiate. It is also an opportunity for the strong to increase the number of channels it uses. Therefore, the strong should consider not only matching the weaker rival's actions, but also making the first move.

CHAPTER TWO

WIDE-AREA BATTLES

OUR SALES DIVISION IS NOW A SHOWPIECE.

BUT COMPANY B ISN'T GOING TO LET THIS RIDE.

THEY'LL RETALIATE SOMEHOW. JUST BECAUSE WE'VE ENGINEERED A REVERSAL, WE CAN'T LET OUR GUARD DOWN.

AND I WANT ALL OF OUR TEAMS TO WORK TOWARD BECOMING NUMBER ONE, LIKE THE SAKAMOTO TEAM.

I'M HOPING THAT THE KONDO, SUZUKI, AND SATO TEAMS WILL FOLLOW THE EXAMPLE SET BY THE SAKAMOTO TEAM.

41

WILL MR. KONDO'S TEAM PREVAIL?

WELL, KNOWING HIM, I GUESS WE DON'T NEED TO WORRY.

DID YOU WANT TO TALK TO ME?

YES, THERE'S SOMEONE I'D LIKE YOU TO MEET.

YOUR GIRLFRIEND?

N-NO! A GUY I WENT TO SCHOOL WITH IS REALLY ANXIOUS TO MEET YOU.

42

HE'S A FOOD WHOLESALER IN NORTHEASTERN JAPAN.

SECTION 3, SALES DIVISION

HE'LL BE IN TOKYO THIS WEEK ON BUSINESS. COULD YOU HAVE DINNER WITH HIM?

HE WANTS TO KNOW ABOUT THE LANCHESTER STRATEGY?

YES. CAN YOU MAKE ROOM IN YOUR SCHEDULE?

LET'S SEE. HOW ABOUT THURSDAY?

THANK YOU. FORGIVE ME FOR ASKING YOU TO DO CONSULTING.

IT'S OKAY. I'M SURE I'LL LEARN SOMETHING, TOO.

YOU AND MATSUDA BOTH LOOK SO YOUNG. WOULD YOU MIND TELLING ME YOUR AGE?

I'M 29. MY FATHER DIED TWO YEARS AGO, AND THAT'S WHY I'M RUNNING THE BUSINESS.

THAT MUST HAVE BEEN HARD FOR YOU.

YES, AT FIRST I WAS TOTALLY ABSORBED IN IT, BUT THINGS HAVE FINALLY SETTLED DOWN.

WE'RE NUMBER ONE IN THE PREFECTURE, AND HAVE MANAGED TO DEFEND OUR POSITION. BUT RECENTLY, A RIVAL RANKING JUST BELOW US LAUNCHED A PRICE WAR.

MATSUDA TOLD ME ABOUT THE LANCHESTER STRATEGY, SO I COUNTERATTACKED WITH A MATCHING OPERATION.

GOOD FOR YOU ...

45

IT WORKED, BUT WHEN I WAS TRYING TO FIGURE OUT A WAY FOR US TO STAY NUMBER ONE ...

I HEARD FROM MATSUDA THAT YOU ARE AN EXPERT ON LANCHESTER STRATEGY, SO THAT'S WHY...

THAT'S RIGHT. MR. SAKAMOTO IS AN EXPERT ON THE LANCHESTER STRATEGY. GO AHEAD, ASK HIM ANYTHING.

CALM DOWN, MATSUDA.

PLEASE GIVE ME SOME ADVICE.

ALL RIGHT. YOUR COMPANY IS NUMBER ONE. IN TERMS OF THE LANCHESTER STRATEGY, THAT PUTS YOU ON THE SIDE OF THE STRONG.

46

THE BASIC STRATEGY FOR THE STRONG IS THE MATCHING OPERATION. YOU USED THAT IN THE PRICE WAR, RIGHT?

THERE ARE FOUR OTHER STRATEGIES: WIDE-AREA BATTLES, STOCHASTIC BATTLES, REMOTE BATTLES, COMPREHENSIVE BATTLES, AND MANIPULATIVE CAMPAIGNS.

HOW ABOUT TRYING A WIDE-AREA BATTLE?

A WIDE-AREA BATTLE IS ONE THAT COVERS A LARGE TERRITORY?

I HEARD ABOUT THAT FROM MATSUDA. AND I READ A BOOK ABOUT IT, BUT ...

OKAY, HERE'S HOW IT WORKS.

47

WIDE-AREA BATTLES

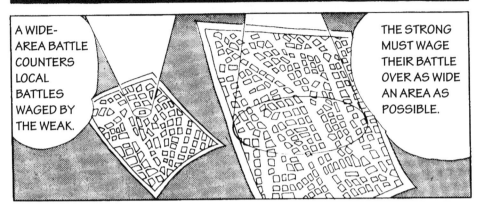

A WIDE-AREA BATTLE COUNTERS LOCAL BATTLES WAGED BY THE WEAK.

THE STRONG MUST WAGE THEIR BATTLE OVER AS WIDE AN AREA AS POSSIBLE.

IF THE BATTLE OF OKEHAZAMA (BETWEEN ODA NOBUNAGA AND IMAGAWA YOSHIMOTO) HAD BEEN FOUGHT ON THE NOBI PLAIN, NOBUNAGA WOULDN'T HAVE HAD A CHANCE.

ALL THAT OPEN SPACE!

IF THE STRONG FIGHT IN A LOCATION WHERE THEY CAN UTILIZE THEIR FORCES EFFECTIVELY, THEIR PROSPECTS OF WINNING INCREASE.

1. WAGE YOUR BATTLE ON AN OPEN FIELD, ON LEVEL GROUND

ON EXPANSES OF FLAT LAND, WHERE CUSTOMERS ARE CONCENTRATED, LARGE MARKETS HAVE ALREADY FORMED AND ARE LINKED TOGETHER ...

SO IT'S HARD TO MAKE A DENT WITH A CONCENTRATED ATTACK ON A SPECIFIC AREA.

YOU HAVE TO ATTACK A LARGE MARKET IN ITS ENTIRETY. THE WEAK DON'T COMPETE WELL IN A BATTLE LIKE THIS BECAUSE THEY LACK COMPREHENSIVE STRENGTH.

SO THE STRONG SHOULD INVEST THEIR STRENGTH IN A LARGE MARKET. IN JAPAN, ALL MAJOR URBAN MARKETS ARE WIDE-AREA BATTLE MARKETS. THE WEAK DON'T HAVE MUCH OF A CHANCE THERE.

2. WAGE YOUR BATTLE IN OPEN TERRITORY OR LOCATION TERRITORY

WHEN WE SPEAK OF FIGHTING A BATTLE ON OPEN TERRITORY, WE MEAN INSTIGATING BATTLES BETWEEN AGENCIES, BASES, OR SALESPEOPLE, WITHOUT SPECIFYING A TERRITORY.

KEY AREA

BY LOCATION TERRITORY, WE MEAN SELECTING A KEY AREA, AND TREATING THE OTHER AREAS AS OPEN TERRITORY.

3. TARGET EASILY SWAYED CUSTOMERS

MR. KOIKE, HOW ABOUT TRYING THE LOCATION TERRITORY STRATEGY?

WELL ...

THAT OCCURRED TO ME WHILE I WAS LISTENING TO YOU.

AS SOON AS I GET BACK, I'LL START MAKING PREPARATIONS.

YOU'VE BEEN A BIG HELP.

GREAT! NOW LET'S GO SOMEWHERE FOR A DRINK.

SURE. MATSUDA, IT'S BEEN A WHILE SINCE I'VE SEEN YOU. YOU'VE CHANGED.

WHAT?

I REALIZED THAT TALKING TO YOU ON THE PHONE THE OTHER DAY. YOU'RE MORE OUTGOING NOW.

IN SCHOOL, YOU WERE QUIET AND INTROVERTED. YOU DIDN'T STAND OUT IN A CROWD

OH, COME ON, NOW ...

I'LL BET YOU'VE BEEN INFLUENCED BY MR. SAKAMOTO.

HA HA HA HA

I'M GOING TO HAVE TO THINK ABOUT REORGANIZING MY COMPANY.

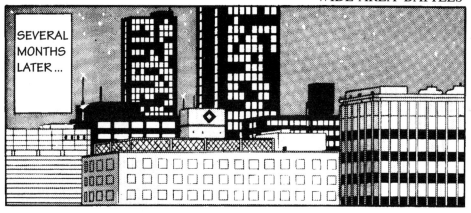

SEVERAL MONTHS LATER...

IS THAT RIGHT? GOOD!

UH, YES, HE'S HERE. JUST A SECOND.

CHIEF, IT'S MR. KOIKE.

WHAT DID HE SAY?

THAT EVERYTHING WORKED OUT FINE.

54

I OWE IT ALL TO YOU, MR. SAKAMOTO. THANKS A MILLION!

I JUST GAVE YOU SOME HINTS. I'LL BET IT WASN'T EASY.

PLEASE COME TO VISIT WITH YOUR FAMILY. I'LL BE HAPPY TO SHOW YOU AROUND.

SOUNDS LIKE A GREAT IDEA. ONE OF THESE DAYS. NEXT TIME YOU'RE IN TOKYO, I'D LIKE TO HEAR THE DETAILS.

I'LL GIVE YOU BACK TO MATSUDA NOW.

THE NEXT DAY ...

DON'T FORGET TO CALL IF YOU NEED ADVICE.

OOOOH...

CHIEF, DID SOMETHING HAPPEN AT THE MEETING?

WELL, KONDO'S STILL HAVING PROBLEMS.

HIS TEAM IS STILL STRUGGLING.

NOW THAT YOU MENTION IT, HE ALWAYS SEEMS TO BE IN A BAD MOOD.

AND HE WON'T LISTEN TO ME, SO ...

AH!

SUGIYAMA, ISN'T ONE OF YOUR FRIENDS ON KONDO'S TEAM?

YES. HE'S REALLY JEALOUS OF OUR TEAM.

DO ME A FAVOR.

WHISPER, WHISPER

WHAT?

TELL MR. KONDO ABOUT THE STRATEGY OF THE WEAK THAT WE'VE BEEN USING?

I THINK THE INFORMATION WILL BE USEFUL TO HIM.

BUT DON'T TELL HIM IT WAS MY IDEA.

I WON'T.

BUT WILL MR. KONDO LISTEN TO WHAT HE SAYS?

I THINK SO. HE'S GRASPING FOR STRAWS NOW. YOU KNOW, WHEN YOU'RE DESPERATE ...

IT'S HARD TO THINK STRAIGHT.

WHY ARE YOU TAKING SUCH AN INTEREST IN KONDO?

HE'S YOUR RIVAL!

I WANT HIM TO GET INTERESTED IN THE LANCHESTER STRATEGY. THAT'S ALL.

58

SUMMARY

A wide-area battle is one that is broad in scope. In a battle of this type, the smaller (weaker) side has no chance of winning, since its small army gets dispersed. Therefore, the weak are likely to choose a small battlefield, a valley, for instance.

This is true of competition between businesses, as well. Weaker players will target a local-battle market, one that is narrow in scope. They might also launch a battle in one, and only one, market.

The strong must not allow the weak to use the strategy of the weak. They must prevent weaker rivals from waging local battles on a limited battlefield, and instead, force them to expand their campaigns.

1. Fighting on plains or on flat land

Markets located on plains or on flat land are bound to be influenced by whatever happens at their centers. Such markets become the scene of wide-area battles. In Japan, the Sapporo, Sendai, Tokyo, Nagoya, Osaka, Hiroshima, and Fukuoka markets fit this description.

A weaker company may launch a local battle in one of these markets by targeting a specific area. However, since these markets are all con-nected, its local battle inevitably turns into a wide-area battle, which it has no hope of winning, no matter how valiant its efforts. Conversely, these are markets in which the strong can use their strength to great advantage, so they should be actively targeting them.

However, the level of share concentration in large markets is generally low. It is difficult to gain an overwhelming lead.

2. Fighting on open or location territory

When we speak of "open territory," we mean territory that is not clearly defined, and in which we sell through any company, at any base, to anyone.

By location territory, we mean a key area that has been pinpointed and mapped out. The territory around it is treated as open territory.

When a manufacturer uses this system, sales companies, agencies, and bases will compete with each other. Its merits are: (1) the manufacturer's market share increases, (2) blind spots decrease, and (3) information-gathering capabilities improve. Consequently, local battles launched by weaker rivals are soon detected.

In a region suited to wide-area battles, it is a good idea to launch a wide-area battle in open territory or location territory, rather than closed territory.

3. Going after customers who follow the crowd

Customers can be divided into two categories: the lone wolves (those who act independently), and those who are easily influenced by what is going on around them. Independent customers have convictions, which is good. They are also stubborn, which can be a problem. So a battle over customers like them is necessarily a local battle.

Battles over the follow-the-crowd customers resemble wide-area battles, since such customers are easily influenced by others. In Japan, there are many of them, since within industrial circles and regions, word of mouth and personal connections have always played an important role. It is easier for companies with large market shares to attack these customers, and we recommend that they do exactly that. The first priority is to win the support of the opinion leaders in the relevant industry or region.

4. Use general-purpose products as your weapons

In a local battle, a weaker rival will segment a customer base, and target one portion of it. It will use a special-purpose product or products as its weapons, which is what it needs to do when waging a local battle.

To retaliate, the stronger company must launch a matching operation. One possibility is to go after a wide-area-type customer base by using a general - purpose product as its weapon. By doing so, the stronger company will be able to eliminate its own blind spots, and leave little room for invasions from weaker rivals. This is a defensive strategy for the strong.

CHAPTER THREE

STOCHASTIC BATTLES

HEY, SAKAMOTO!

RATTLE RATTLE

OH, MR. ONO! IT'S BEEN A WHILE.

WE'RE BOTH SO BUSY WE HARDLY EVER SEE EACH OTHER.

GLUB,
GLUB

GLUB,
GLUB

THERE'S
NOTHING LIKE
THE FIRST
GLASS OF
BEER!

ESPECIALLY
AFTER A
WORKOUT!

BUT THEN YOU GET HUNGRY AND START WORRYING ABOUT YOUR WEIGHT.

THEN YOU CAN EXERCISE SOME MORE.

MY WIFE STARTED DOING JAZZ DANCE. SHE'S THRILLED BECAUSE SHE THINKS SHE'S LOST A LITTLE WEIGHT.

ANYWAY, HERE'S WHAT I WANTED TO ASK YOU.

AFTER OUR GREAT SUCCESS, WHICH I OWE TO YOU, WE PUT OUT TWO NEW SPECIAL-PURPOSE PRODUCTS. THEY'VE BOTH BECOME NUMBER ONE IN THE INDUSTRY.

WOW! THAT'S AMAZING.

BUT COMPANY C IS DEVELOPING PRODUCTS THAT ARE THE SAME AS OURS.

I'M NOT SURPRISED. YOU'VE GOT TO EXPECT YOUR RIVALS TO FIGHT BACK.

IF COMPANY C STARTS SELLING PRODUCTS THAT TARGET THE SAME USERS ...

THAT WILL STIMULATE THE MARKET, AND YOU SHOULD BENEFIT SINCE YOU'RE IN A STRONG POSITION.

YOU MEAN THAT IF COMPANY C STARTS DOING DIFFERENTIATION, WE SHOULD COME OUT WITH SIMILAR PRODUCTS?

YES. YOU NEED TO FIND OUT WHAT KIND OF PRODUCTS COMPANY C IS PLANNING AS SOON AS POSSIBLE.

YOUR NEXT MOVE SHOULD BE A STOCHASTIC BATTLE. THE IDEA IS TO CREATE NUMBER ONES FROM YOUR TOP-RANKING POSITION.

STOCHASTIC BATTLE?

STOCHASTIC BATTLES

STOCHASTIC BATTLES COUNTERACT THE SINGLE COMBAT OF THE WEAK. THE STRONG SHOULD AVOID SINGLE COMBAT. THEY HAVE NUMERICAL STRENGTH, AND SHOULD USE IT.

RETREAT IS VICTORY!

IN SAMURAI BATTLES, EVEN THE MOST SKILLED SWORDSMAN CAN'T WIN IF HE'S FACED WITH THREE OR MORE OPPONENTS AT THE SAME TIME.

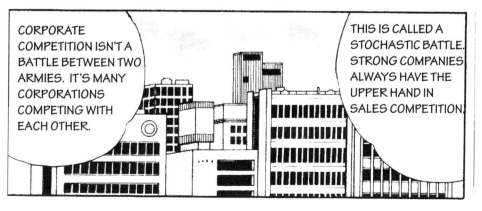

CORPORATE COMPETITION ISN'T A BATTLE BETWEEN TWO ARMIES. IT'S MANY CORPORATIONS COMPETING WITH EACH OTHER.

THIS IS CALLED A STOCHASTIC BATTLE. STRONG COMPANIES ALWAYS HAVE THE UPPER HAND IN SALES COMPETITION.

1. FORTIFY YOUR PRODUCT LINE

2. ENCOURAGE YOUR AGENCIES, YOUR OWN BASES, AND SALESPEOPLE TO COMPETE WITH EACH OTHER

68

SIX
MONTHS
LATER...

YEAH, THAT'S HIM, ALL RIGHT.

MR. ONO! HOW NICE TO SEE YOU.

AH, SAKAMOTO! WHAT LUCK! WHAT ARE YOU DOING HERE?

I'M RUNNING A TECHNICAL TRAINING SESSION FOR OUR USERS.

THAT'S A LOT OF WORK.

WE'RE CELEBRATING OUR COMPANY'S TWENTIETH ANNIVERSARY.

OH? CONGRATU-LATIONS!

HOW ABOUT MAKING AN APPEARANCE?

OH, THANK YOU.

WE HAVE HOSTESSES IN BUNNY OUTFITS.

A-AGAIN?!

DID YOU SOLVE YOUR PROBLEM?

OH, YES. I'LL TELL YOU ALL ABOUT IT NEXT CHANCE I GET.

COMPANY C DID TRY DIFFERENTIATION ...

WE COURTED ONE OF THEIR DRONES ...

WHO GAVE US INFORMATION, AND WE WERE ABLE TO MATCH THEM RIGHT AWAY.

THIS MORNING WE HAD A SALES MEETING. OUR USER-SPECIFIC PRODUCTS ARE FLYING OFF THE SHELVES.

THAT'S GREAT NEWS!

OUR LADIES' OFFENSIVE HAS BEEN A BIG HIT, TOO. I OWE IT ALL TO YOU.

MR. PRESIDENT, IT'S TIME TO ...

OK, BE RIGHT WITH YOU.

SEE YOU, SAKAMOTO. I'LL BE THANKING YOU PROPERLY SOON.

SO LONG TILL THEN.

74

GOODBYE. SEE YOU AT THE CLUB.

MR. SAKAMOTO, YOU REALLY GET AROUND, DON'T YOU!

I'LL BET YOU GAVE HIM ADVICE ABOUT THE LANCHESTER STRATEGY.

HE SEEMED SO GRATEFUL. I'LL BET HE'S GOING TO REWARD YOU HANDSOMELY.

NAH, HE'S THE TYPE WHO TENDS TO FORGET ABOUT SUCH THINGS.

OH, BEFORE I FORGET, THE KONDO TEAM SEEMS TO BE DOING BETTER, THANKS TO SUGIYAMA.

OH? GOOD, I WAS WORRIED.

KONDO IS HIS OLD SELF ONCE AGAIN

SAKAMOTO, I CAN DO ANYTHING!

THIS IS THE FIRST TIME I'VE SEEN MR. KONDO WORK SO HARD ...

IF MR. SAKAMOTO AND MR. KONDO WORKED TOGETHER, NOBODY COULD BEAT THEM ...

NEXT YEAR IS COMPANY W'S 30TH ANNIVERSARY. THEY'RE AIMING FOR OVERALL NUMBER-ONE STATUS.

IT'S TIME FOR THE TRAINING SEMINAR.

OKAY. LET'S GIVE IT ALL WE'VE GOT.

SUMMARY

Stochastic battles make use of "stochastic" weapons, e.g., machine guns. The combatants do not face each other one-to-one. In such battles, probability is a major factor, and according to Lanchester's Second Law, the army with greater numerical strength has an overwhelming edge.

A strong army must avoid man-to-man combat, and instead overpower the weaker army with its numerical strength. About the swordfights that used to occur in Japan, it was said that even the most skilled swordsman could not win if attacked by three opponents at the same time. In the Pacific War, U.S. fighter plane squadrons had a high success rate because they flew in teams.

Wars are usually struggles between two enemies, but in the business world, we have many corporations competing with each other. This is a stochastic battle. Consequently, a strong company is in an extremely advantageous position, for the following reasons:

(1) When there are a lot of competitors, customers are likely to become confused. However, the probability that the customer will choose a strong company on the basis of its past performance, its name recognition, i.e., because of its reliability, is very high.

(2) Since weaker companies are also competing with each other, they tend to wear each other out. This is one reason for the widening of gaps between companies that we are seeing today.

Therefore, a strong company will want to invest its energy in markets where there is a lot of competition, or where customers are apt to conduct similar transactions with more than one company. The strong might even want to go one step further, and encourage intra-company competition, thus eliminating blind spots, and preventing the weak from encroaching on their territory.

1. Expand your product line

   Manufacturers might increase the number of products they make, so that they can market a robust product line. If their own products are competing with each other, there is no room for the weak to erode their profits. This can be accomplished to a certain extent with a series of matching operations, which will offset weaker competitors' attempts at product differentiation. However, the ultimate goal should be expanding the product line.

2. Increase your inventory

   Retailers, wholesalers, and service industries need to increase their inventories. By doing so, you will eliminate blind spots and convince customers that you stock everything they could possibly want.

3. Pit your agencies against each other

   Manufacturers and trading companies would do well to use a great many agencies. You will be creating open territory and, thus, competition between your agencies.

   If in addition to primary wholesalers, you have secondary and even tertiary wholesalers, in other words, if you deal with a large number of middlemen, you're engaging in a stochastic battle. This is particularly important today, when many wholesalers make exaggerated claims, but don't produce. Unless they are forced to compete, their performance won't improve.

4. Encourage competition within your company or among your stores

   When you encourage competition among your own sales divisions or stores, you are fighting a stochastic battle.

Strong companies must make an active effort to acquire as many customers as possible, at every base, and at every store. In the retail and service sectors, strong companies in a particular region are often those that are based there. They may be threatened when a weaker rival with a nationwide operation attempts to infiltrate their territory. When that happens, a strong company often attempts to counter the invasion by launching an emotional local battle against a nationwide chain, for instance. However, it is better, in a case like this, to fight a stochastic battle by banding together with other stores in the area, surrounding the enemy invader.

CHAPTER FOUR

REMOTE BATTLES

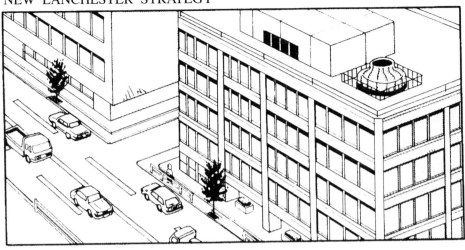

I'VE RECEIVED PROPOSALS FROM THREE SECTIONS ABOUT CREATING NUMBER ONES. LET'S HEAR THEM NOW.

THIS IS SAKAMOTO'S PROPOSAL, SO I'D LIKE HIM TO EXPLAIN IT.

REMOTE BATTLES

REMOTE BATTLES ARE USED TO COUNTER CLOSE COMBAT, A STRATEGY OF THE WEAK.

THE STRONG CAN USE THEIR POWER TO ADVANTAGE WHEN THEY WAGE THEIR BATTLES FROM A DISTANCE.

EVEN A GRAND CHAMPION SUMO WRESTLER CANNOT EXERT HIS FULL STRENGTH IF AN OPPONENT GETS TOO CLOSE TO HIM.

THIS IS A GOOD DISTANCE.

BUT SALES STRATEGY, UNLIKE A MILITARY BATTLE, IS A BATTLE FOR CUSTOMERS. A REMOTE BATTLE TAKES PLACE FAR AWAY FROM THE CUSTOMERS.

1. MAKE FULL USE OF WHOLESALERS

WEAK MANUFACTURERS ARE BETTER OFF DOING DIRECT SALES, BUT THE STRONG SHOULD MAKE FULL USE OF WHOLESALERS.

THE STRONG CAN DO THIS SIMPLY BECAUSE OF THEIR STRENGTH.

YOU'LL ACQUIRE ADDED STRENGTH IF YOU USE MANY WHOLESALERS AS EXTENSIONS OF YOUR COMPANY.

2. DO MORE PUBLICITY AND ADVERTISING

PUBLICITY AND ADVERTISING ARE REMOTE BATTLES, TOO.

TOP-RANKING COMPANIES WITH HIGH PROFILES MUST IMPROVE THEIR IMAGES EVEN MORE.

THE "IMAGE" IS INVISIBLE, BUT IT CARRIES A LOT OF POWER.

TO DO THAT, YOU NEED TO ADVERTISE, BUT NOT ON A SMALL SCALE.

SO, WHAT IS IT THAT WE SHOULD DO?

I'LL START BY TALKING ABOUT CONCENTRATING MORE ON INDIRECT SALES.

APPARENTLY, THE SAFEST METHOD IS TO ENGAGE IN 50% DIRECT SALES AND 50% INDIRECT SALES.

WE HAD BEEN POURING OUR ENERGY INTO DIRECT SALES, BECAUSE WE WERE IN A WEAK POSITION, SO OUR RATIO WAS 60-40.

NOW WE SHOULD PUT MORE EMPHASIS ON INDIRECT SALES. THAT MEANS INCREASING THE NUMBER OF AGENCIES WE USE.

WHAT DOES THE LANCHESTER STRATEGY TELL US ABOUT WHICH AGENCIES TO GO AFTER?

MOST OF THE AGENCIES WE USE NOW ARE WHOLESALERS WITH NATIONAL OR WIDE-AREA NETWORKS.

THAT MAKES SENSE, BECAUSE IN OUR STRONG POSITION, WE SHOULD BE FIGHTING A WIDE-AREA BATTLE.

ANOTHER STRATEGY FOR THE STRONG IS THE STOCHASTIC BATTLE. THIS INVOLVES GETTING OUR AGENCIES TO COMPETE WITH EACH OTHER, THUS DECREASING OUR BLIND SPOTS AND INCREASING OUR MARKET SHARE.

IF THERE IS NO COMPETITION AMONG OUR AGENCIES, THEN THEY'LL BECOME COMPLACENT, AND WON'T WORK HARD FOR US.

THAT'S RIGHT.

SO WHICH AGENCY SHOULD WE CHOOSE TO COMPETE WITH OUR NATIONAL WHOLESALERS?

HOW ABOUT THE NUMBER-ONE WHOLE-SALER IN A REGION?

BUT CREATING A NUMBER-ONE REGION IS A STRATEGY FOR THE WEAK, ISN'T IT?

YES. BUT THE GOAL OF THE STRONG MUST BE CREATING A NUMBER-ONE PRODUCT. TO DO THAT, THEY HAVE TO CREATE A NUMBER-ONE WHOLESALER.

BUT IT'S REALLY HARD TO BECOME NUMBER ONE WITH A NATIONAL WHOLESALER.*

THAT'S RIGHT. THEY'RE PRETTY FUSSY ABOUT WHAT THEY STOCK.

*THIS MEANS THAT THE WHOLESALER'S SUPPLY RATE IS AHEAD OF THE NEAREST COMPETITOR BY A FACTOR OF 3:1.

THAT'S NO REASON TO GIVE UP, BUT LET'S TALK ABOUT HOW TO BECOME NUMBER ONE IN THE NATION.

I THINK THAT TO SUPPRESS THE WEAK WE HAVE TO USE A WHOLESALER THAT'S NUMBER ONE IN ITS REGION.

BUT DON'T WIDE-AREA WHOLESALERS HAVE MORE SELLING POWER THAN REGIONAL WHOLESALERS?

MARKET SHARE IS MORE IMPORTANT THAN SALES

I THINK WE NEED TO INVESTIGATE THIS SOME MORE.

90

NEXT, ABOUT BOOSTING OUR PUBLICITY AND ADVERTISING CAMPAIGNS ...

NOW THAT WE'RE NUMBER ONE, WE HAVE TO RAISE OUR CORPORATE IMAGE.

WE SHOULD PLACE ADS IN INDUSTRY AND TRADE PUBLICATIONS EMPHASIZING THE FACT THAT COMPANY W IS NUMBER ONE.

FOCUS ON RISING COMPANIES COMPANY W STRONG, STEADY, SURE GROWTH

COMPANY W IS #1

YES, WE SHOULD.

NO ONE SEEMS TO OBJECT.

I'LL HAVE TO SEE HOW MUCH WE CAN BUDGET FOR THIS.

I AGREE.

THAT'LL BE ALL FOR TODAY. I'LL HEAR A REPORT ON THE REGIONAL WHOLESALER MATTER AT THE NEXT MANAGERS' MEETING.

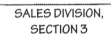

SALES DIVISION, SECTION 3

THAT'S GOOD NEWS ABOUT KONDO'S TEAM, ISN'T IT.

YES. THANKS, SUGIYAMA!

?

CHIEF, WHAT'S THIS ABOUT KONDO?

92

I JUST GAVE HIM A LITTLE HINT. HE'S GOT WHAT IT TAKES, YOU KNOW.

NEVER MIND THAT. WE'VE GOT TO MAKE THIS COMPANY NUMBER ONE!

YES, SIR!

KITCHEN

MR. SAKAMOTO IS SO AMAZING!

RUMIKO'S IN A GOOD MOOD THESE DAYS.

93

94

I'M THE ONE WHO MADE THIS COMPANY NUMBER ONE, YOU KNOW.

YOU'RE ALWAYS TALKING ABOUT SAKAMOTO, AND I DON'T LIKE IT.

UH, THANK YOU.

HERE!

PUT A LITTLE MORE MILK IN NEXT TIME, OK?

SEE YOU!

WHY'D HE HAVE TO COME IN HERE?

BUT MR. KONDO DESERVES SOME CREDIT. HE REALLY WORKED HARD.

I HAVE MORE RESPECT FOR HIM NOW.

CONFERENCE
ROOM NO. 3

NOW LET'S TALK ABOUT THE PROPOSAL SUBMITTED BY SECTION 3 AT THE SALES MEETING.

YOU MUST ALL HAVE BEEN THINKING ABOUT IT, SO LET'S HEAR WHAT YOU HAVE TO SAY.

I THINK IT'S A GOOD IDEA. FROM NOW ON, WE'LL NEED TO FOCUS ON REGIONS.

IF THAT'S OUR GOAL, I THINK A NUMBER-ONE REGIONAL WHOLESALER IS THE WAY TO GO.

I AGREE, BUT I DON'T LIKE THE IDEA OF CHOOSING A WHOLESALER WITH A LOW VOLUME.

NEITHER DO I. I THINK WE'D BE BETTER OFF GOING WITH COMPANY F, WITH ITS STRONGER SELLING POWER, THAN WITH COMPANY E.

COMPANY E COVERS ONLY ONE PREFECTURE. COMPANY F COVERS A WIDER AREA, SO OF COURSE IT LOOKS BETTER.

BUT COMPANY E HAS A MUCH BIGGER MARKET SHARE.

OHASHI, YOU KEEP TALKING ABOUT MARKET SHARE ...

BUT IF WE TAKE AN OVERALL COMPANY VIEWPOINT, REVENUE COMES FIRST. WE SHOULD CHOOSE NATIONAL OR WIDE-AREA WHOLESALERS.

NOW THAT WE'RE IN A POSITION OF STRENGTH, CAN'T WE USE A LOT OF AGENCIES?

VERY WELL.

SAKAMOTO, WE'VE GOT A DECISION ON THE AGENCY MATTER.

OUR SUGGESTION HAS BEEN ADOPTED.

IT HAS?!

GREAT! I WAS WORRIED.

99

THEN, HOW ABOUT USING COMPANY D AS OUR MAIN AGENCY?

WE DON'T HAVE TO DO IT RIGHT AWAY, BUT WE SHOULD MAKE PREPARATIONS.

HOW ABOUT ADVERTISING?

WE'VE FOUND OUT THAT THE BEST THING TO DO IS TO PLACE ADS IN TWO INDUSTRY MAGAZINES AND A TRADE PAPER.

SINCE OUR MARKET SHARE AND SALES HAVE RISEN, OUR EXECUTIVES ARE MORE WILLING TO SPEND MONEY NOW.

100

SINCE KONDO'S TEAM HAS FINALLY MANAGED TO ENGINEER A REVERSAL, WE'LL BE NUMBER ONE SOON.

.....

CHIEF?

I CAN'T GET MY MIND OFF COMPANY B.

WHAT IS IT?

NOTHING SPECIAL. IT'S JUST THAT ...

MR. OHASHI, YOU'RE JUST A WORRY WART.

IT'LL BE OK. WE'RE WITH YOU ALL THE WAY.

WE INVITED AGENCIES FROM ALL OVER JAPAN TO A CONFERENCE AT A HOT SPRING RESORT, REMEMBER?

YES. THREE OF OUR PEOPLE ATTENDED.

ACCOUNTING CLAIMS THAT OUR TEAM SPENT TOO MUCH ON PHONE CALLS.

THAT CAN'T BE HELPED, THOUGH.

YOU'RE ALL BEING MANIPULATED LONG-DISTANCE BY YOUR WIVES.

103

Summary

Remote battles are used as counterattacks against the close-combat strategy adopted by the weak. The weak choose close combat because it is a type of warfare in which the strong cannot exploit their strength. Close combat also helps the weak to detect the shortcomings of the strong.

The strong, however, must fight their battles from a distance. They can then observe the battle zone objectively, and use their strength to full advantage.

However, unlike a military battle, sales strategy is a battle for customers. Therefore, a remote battle is a battle fought far away from the customer, rather than a battle fought far away from the enemy.

Specifically, a remote battle involves a manufacturer's using primary and secondary agencies, a primary agency's using a secondary agency; or a secondary agency's using a tertiary agency. For the retail and service industries, in-store sales is a close combat. (Outside and mail-order sales are remote battle).

However, to win today, you must reach the end user. Retailers and services know how lazy customers have become. Therefore, you must be careful how you launch your remote battle, and you must know when to use the remote-battle strategy and when to use the close-combat strategy.

1. Make full use of your wholesalers

Strong manufacturers should make full use of their primary and secondary wholesalers to counter direct sales campaigns launched by weaker rivals. Wholesalers, of course, want to handle merchandise that is easy to sell, so they are bound to be enthusiastic about supporting the products of a leading, well known company.

When manufacturers can rely on the strength of their wholesalers, not just their own strength, they can compete in many more markets, and increase their sales volume. They can do this by virtue of their strength so, again, they should make good use of primary and secondary wholesalers.

One caveat, though: avoid indiscriminately increasing the number of agencies you deal with. We will discuss this subject later, but the desired direct-indirect ratio is 50-50. (The current national average is 30% direct vs. 70% indirect so, as you can see, indirect sales carries greater weight in today's business world.) If you have too many agencies, you may lose control of them, which would wreak havoc with the market.

Deciding what to do about indirect sales is always a problem. In today's business climate, the most important strategy is regional strategy. Both the strong and the weak are striving to create number-one regions.

The weak will focus on the number-one wholesaler in a particular region in their efforts to create a number-one region. Therefore, the strong should make the first move by using regional wholesalers as well as national ones.

The same theory applies to the use of primary stores. Retailers and the service industries must act to ensure that customers will patronize their stores. This mean that in addition to conducting steamroller PR and canvassing campaigns, and distributing flyers and direct mail, they must also put more effort into outside sales.

2. Put more emphasis on advertising and publicity

Advertising and publicity are also remote battles. A strong company with a proven track record and a high profile needs to reinforce its image through media ads (television, newspapers, and magazines). It must convince the public that its products are the best.

Images are invisible, but they carry a tremendous amount of influence. Already high images can be enhanced by advertising and publicity. Though advertising and publicity are not as effective as they once were, they can still establish a company's image. If you are number one, and there is a huge gap between you and number two, you will find that easy to do.

However, though a strong company's advertising campaigns will necessarily be more effective than those of a weak company, the former must be careful not to spread their campaigns too thinly. Concentration is everything.

Distribution Channel Strategy

The two decisions a manufacturer must make about its distribution channel strategy are as follows:

(1) What the direct-indirect ratio should be
(2) What the focus of indirect sales should be

The direct-indirect ratio

A 50-50 ratio is viewed as a stable one, because

In good times, indirect sales are more effective. In a recession, direct sales makes more sense.

Indirect sales works better for growth products or in a growth market; direct sales is more effective for well established products or in a mature market

Indirect sales is for the strong; direct sales is for the weak.

We don't expect an economic boom for quite some time, but manufacturers have both growth and mature products in their lines, and both strong and weak companies have products on the market. Every company's sales territory includes both growth and mature markets.

In other words, with a direct-indirect sales ratio of 50-50, you can adapt to any situation. However, in Japan, manufacturers generally opt for a ratio of 30-70, which means that they are relying too heavily on indirect sales. It would be useful for them to increase the direct-sales portion of this ratio, but they must be careful to limit themselves to particular regions, products, or routes during the process.

Distribution Stages

As far as the focus of indirect sales is concerned, first let us touch upon the various distribution stages (or how the product goes from the manufacturer to the consumer or user), using N to represent the number of stages.

When a manufacturer engages in direct sales to the consumer or user, there are zero stages. When the manufacturer sells to the consumer through a retailer, or to the user through a wholesaler, there is one stage.

Here are the factors that govern N.

Number of retailers and users and their geographical distribution

When the numbers are high and the area is large, N increases

The degree of value added to merchandise

When this is high, N can be decreased.

Market share

When this is large, N can be made larger.

Strategy

When a manufacturer attempts to control its distribution channels, N becomes smaller. When it entrusts that task to others, N becomes larger. However, since in today's world the company that captures the end user is in a stronger position, it is a good idea to keep N as small as possible.

Push and Pull Strategies

Now we will discuss the "push" and "pull" strategies. Push, in this context, describes a strategy that goes from upstream to downstream.

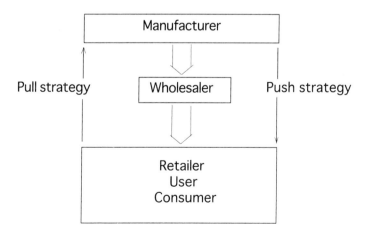

First, the manufacturer encourages wholesalers to accept more orders. Consequently, wholesalers work harder to sell to retailers and users, and retailers, in turn, make more of an effort to sell to consumers. The push strategy is a strategy for the strong, and requires support and guidance from the manufacturer.

The pull strategy goes from downstream to upstream. First the manufacturer encourages consumers or users to buy its products. Consequently, consumers or users make it known to retailers and wholesalers that they wish to buy the manufacturer's products. Therefore, retailers increase their orders to wholesalers, and wholesalers place more orders with manufacturers.

The pull strategy is a strategy for the weak, and with it comes the necessity to educate customers and users through advertising and publicity.

The decision about which strategy to use is determined by your market share and the idiosyncrasies of the relevant territory.

It is a good idea, when planning your distribution channel strategy, to keep the points outlined above in mind. Please remember, though, that the purpose of distribution channels is to increase your market share. Today, when there is so much emphasis on regional strategy, it is best to reinforce channels in regions where you would like to raise your market share. In other words, base your distribution channel strategy on your regional strategy.

CHAPTER FIVE

COMPREHENSIVE   BATTLES

SECTION 3'S STRUGGLE CONTINUES.

THE TEAM HAS TO OUTPERFORM THE OTHER TEAMS.

THANKS! LINE 3, RIGHT?

HOW ARE YOU DOING? I'M SORRY I HAVEN'T BEEN ABLE TO RETURN YOUR CALLS.

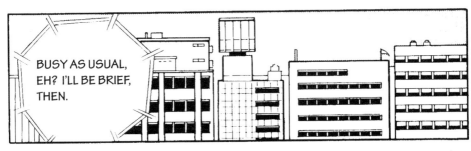

BUSY AS USUAL, EH? I'LL BE BRIEF, THEN.

I NEED TO TALK TO YOU. CAN WE MEET SOMETIME THIS WEEK?

SATURDAY NIGHT? HOW ABOUT 8:00? SURE, I KNOW WHERE IT IS.

SEE YOU THEN.

WONDER WHAT THIS IS ABOUT. HIS BUSINESS, I GUESS ...

CHIEF, MR. KATAYAMA RUNS A FAMILY RESTAURANT, DOESN'T HE?

THANK YOU.

THAT'S RIGHT. HE INVITED ALL OF US THERE A WHILE AGO FOR BARBECUED BEEF, REMEMBER?

THE FOOD WAS REALLY GOOD. EVERYONE WANTS TO GO BACK AGAIN.

LET'S DO THAT. I FELT SORRY FOR HIM — THERE WERE SO MANY OF US.

HA, HA, HA!

WE KEPT HIM BUSY!

THANKS FOR COMING. I'VE RESERVED A TABLE OVER THERE.

WHAT DID YOU WANT TO TALK ABOUT?

ACTUALLY, IT'S NOT ABOUT MY PROBLEMS THIS TIME.

HUH?

THIS IS MY FRIEND HAMADA. HE OWNS A SUPERMARKET IN THE X AREA.

HOW DO YOU DO? THANK YOU FOR TAKING TIME OUT FROM YOUR BUSY SCHEDULE.

HOW DO YOU DO? I'M SAKAMOTO.

I'VE HEARD A LOT ABOUT YOU FROM KATAYAMA. I HAVE A FAVOR TO ASK YOU.

SORRY ABOUT THAT.

I RUN A SUPERMARKET WITH MY FATHER-IN-LAW. WE'RE NUMBER ONE IN OUR AREA

BUT RECENTLY THE NO. 2 STORE HAS UNDERGONE A COMPLETE RENEWAL. THEY'RE STOCKING MUCH LESS CLOTHING, FOCUSING ON PRODUCE, MEAT, AND FISH.

KATAYAMA SAYS THAT WHAT THEY'RE DOING SOUNDS LIKE "ONE-POINT CONCENTRATION" FROM THE LANCHESTER STRATEGY FOR THE WEAK.

SO WE'RE MATCHING THEM BY FOCUSING ON THE SAME MERCHANDISE, BUT THEY'VE MANAGED TO GET THEIR NAME OUT THERE ....

THEIR ADS SAY THAT THEY'RE THE ONLY COMPANY TO BUY THESE ITEMS FROM, SO WE'VE GOT AN UPHILL BATTLE ON OUR HANDS.

I TOLD HAMADA THAT IF THE ENEMY'S USING THE LANCHESTER STRATEGY, HIS COMPANY SHOULD, TOO.

THAT'S RIGHT. SO, MR. SAKAMOTO...

THAT EXPLAINS WHY I ASKED YOU TO MEET ME TONIGHT.

I COULDN'T STAND SEEING A BIG GUY LIKE HAMADA LOOKING SO HOPELESS.

I'D REALLY LIKE TO HELP HIM.

WELL, WE'RE HAVING A ROUGH TIME, TOO, EVEN THOUGH WE'RE IN A STRONG POSITION. I DON'T KNOW ...

BUT YOU MIGHT TRY A COMPREHENSIVE BATTLE. THAT MIGHT WORK.

COMPRE-HENSIVE BATTLE?

COMPREHENSIVE BATTLES

COMPREHENSIVE BATTLES ARE FOUGHT TO COUNTERACT WEAKER RIVALS' ONE-POINT CONCENTRATION

IN A BATTLE LIKE THIS, THE STRONG ARMY SHOULD USE ALL THE WEAPONS IT'S GOT.

IN A REAL WAR, THE STRONG ARMY MOBILIZES ITS LAND, SEA, AND AIR FORCES TO DESTROY THE WEAK. THIS IS A COMPREHENSIVE BATTLE.

EVEN IF A STRONG COMPANY HAS WEAK POINTS, IT CAN COVER FOR THEM IN OTHER WAYS.

STRONG COMPANIES SHOULD USE THEIR STRENGTH, AIMING FOR A SYNERGISTIC EFFECT.

IN SALES STRATEGY, IT'S IMPORTANT FOR THE STRONG TO COMBINE THE STRENGTH OF THEIR PRODUCTS, SALESMANSHIP, SALES PROMOTION, AND IMAGE.

PRODUCT STRENGTH

SALESMANSHIP

SALES PROMOTION STRENGTH

IMAGE

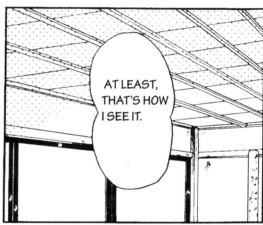

AT LEAST, THAT'S HOW I SEE IT.

I THINK YOU NEED TO USE ALL OF YOUR STRONG POINTS: THE SIZE OF YOUR STORES, YOUR INVENTORY, YOUR REPUTATION.

120

I'LL KEEP YOU POSTED.

HE'S ALWAYS BEEN A LITTLE WEIRD.

BY THE WAY, HOW'S KATAYAMA DOING?

REALLY WELL.

WOW! THAT'S GREAT!

RECENTLY HE OPENED BRANCHES THAT OFFER JAPANESE AND CHINESE CUISINE.

AND LISTEN TO THIS. HE GIVES CUSTOMERS MINIATURE COMPUTERS AND HAS THEM INPUT THEIR ORDERS INTO THEM.

THE ORDER GOES DIRECTLY TO THE KITCHEN. KIDS LOVE THE IDEA BECAUSE THEY'RE REMINDED OF THEIR HOME COMPUTERS.

HI-TECH HAS COME TO OUR BUSINESS, TOO.

HMM, THAT IS A GOOD IDEA.

AND HOW ARE YOU DOING? YOU SAID YOU'VE BEEN HAVING A ROUGH TIME.

YEAH, THAT'S RIGHT.

GOOD LUCK! IF YOU CAN'T DO IT, NOBODY CAN.

OH, BY THE WAY, HOW ABOUT HAVING A REUNION WITH SOME OF OUR COLLEGE BUDDIES?

GREAT IDEA! LET'S DO IT!

THEY ALL WANT TO HEAR WHAT YOU'VE GOT TO SAY.

HEY, KATAYAMA! THIS HAS GOT TO STOP!

HA! HA! HA!

123

TWO MONTHS LATER ...

REALLY? GLAD TO HEAR IT.

I WENT BACK TO MY HOTEL AND STARTED THINKING. I DECIDED TO ENLARGE MY FOOD SECTION TO √3 TIMES THE SIZE OF COMPANY A'S.

SO I WAS ABLE TO OFFER MORE VARIETY.

124

I RAN A COMMERCIAL ON A LOCAL TV STATION, AND HAD FLYERS MADE, WHICH WE HAND- DISTRIBUTED.

THE FLYERS REALLY PAID OFF. I REALIZE THAT I'D BEEN HOPING FOR SUCCESS, BUT WASN'T MAKING MUCH OF AN EFFORT ON MY PART.

NOW I KNOW THAT IT TAKES HARD WORK.

YES. WE'VE BEEN USING LOCAL WHOLESALERS IN ADDITION TO NATIONAL AND WIDE-AREA WHOLESALERS.

BUT THEY'RE SMALL, AND THERE ARE SO MANY OF THEM! THEY'RE WORKING HARD FOR US, BUT ...

I KNOW WHAT YOU MEAN.

I'VE SET UP A DELIVERY SYSTEM. CUSTOMERS HAVE GOTTEN LAZY, SO I THOUGHT IT MIGHT CATCH ON.

IT DID. THE RESPONSE HAS BEEN *GOOD*, ESPECIALLY FROM MARRIED WOMEN WHO WORK AND FROM OLDER PEOPLE.

I OWE ALL OF THIS TO YOU. THANK YOU SO MUCH.

NO, NO, IT MUST HAVE BEEN YOUR DETERMINATION.

I HAVE ANOTHER QUESTION FOR YOU.

WHAT? OK, LET'S HEAR IT.

I'M CHAIRMAN OF THE LOCAL CHAMBER OF COMMERCE, SO I CAN'T GO AROUND TALKING ABOUT COMPETITION.

THAT'S STARTING TO BE A PROBLEM.

THE PUBLIC POSITION OF THE STRONG MUST BE "WE'RE IN THE SAME BUSINESS, SO WE SHOULD WORK TOGETHER." YOU HAVE TO EMPHASIZE COEXISTENCE ...

ACTUALLY, IT'S THE WEAK YOU HAVE TO ATTACK. YOU SHOULD NEVER UTTER THE WORD "SHARE," IN PUBLIC, THOUGH.

ASSUMING THAT KIND OF ATTITUDE AT THE CHAMBER OF COMMERCE IS ONE TYPE OF COMPREHENSIVE BATTLE, YOU SHOULD HAVE SOME SORT OF EXCUSE READY TO EXPLAIN YOUR RECENT ACTIVITIES.

YES. I SEE WHAT YOU MEAN.

I'LL BE GOING NOW. SORRY TO LEAVE SO ABRUPTLY ...

I'VE GOT AN IDEA, AND I WANT TO GET TO WORK ON IT RIGHT AWAY.

BUT YOU HAVEN'T FINISHED YOUR MEAL!

I'LL PAY THE BILL ON MY WAY OUT. PLEASE TAKE YOUR TIME.

....

SUMMARY

Comprehensive battles are those in which armies mobilize all their forces and weapons. The weaker army (in terms of comprehensive strength) will focus all its forces on one particular area. The stronger army, on the other hand, will counter the enemy's efforts by using all its weapons, and will attempt to win with its overwhelming numerical superiority.

In war, the stronger army will mobilize its land, sea, and air forces to destroy the enemy. This is a comprehensive battle. Even if there are holes in its armor, so to speak, the stronger army can make up for them otherwise, since the impact it makes expands not arithmetically, but exponentially.

In other words, a comprehensive battle allows the stronger army to take full advantage of its strength.

In business competition, as well, market leaders must fight comprehensive battles. There are two aspects to this type of battle – defense and offense.

Defense

If, for instance, a weaker rival launches a concentrated offense on a key region, the stronger company must not only respond to that attack with its overwhelming strength, but also launch its own attack in another region. Then, the weaker rival will be put on the defensive, and will have to discontinue its one-point concentration campaign.

Similarly, when a weaker rival launches a concentrated attack on a key product or customer base, the stronger company should use its overwhelming strength to foil that attack. It must also attack another product or customer base.

The same strategy applies to direct mail, flyers, and floor space where retailers and the service industries are concerned.

Again, when a weaker rival launches a concentrated offense on a key product or customer base, the stronger company need only assume a defensive position backed up by its superior resources, and launch its own offensive against other products or customer bases.

The same goes for direct mail, flyers, and floor space in the retail and service industries.

The comprehensive battle is a strategy for the strong, since it does not allow the weak to use the one-point concentration strategy effectively.

By "overwhelming strength," we mean that you are ahead of your weaker rival by a factor of $\sqrt{3}$ (see Volume 1).

Offense

For corporations, there are two types of war potential – product strength and sales strength.

By product strength, we mean

Quality and performance
Price
Variety
Product image

Sales strength is a matter of

(For manufacturers and wholesalers)

Size and quality of sales force (offensive quantity)
After-market service
Corporate image

(For retailers and the service industries)

Store quality
Corporate (store) image
Quantity and quality of direct mail and flyers
Floor space and business hours

The strong need to use these weapons to the maximum, aiming for a synergistic effect. Your results will be exponentially better if, when you advertise, you run publicity campaigns and hand-distribute flyers at the same time your commercials are shown on television. To win, you must ensure that the quality and performance of your products, sales force, and store employees are at least equal to those of your weaker rival. The size of your product line and your sales force, and the amount of direct mail and flyers you distribute must exceed those of your weaker rival by at least a factor of $\sqrt{3}$. The synergistic effect is a good one for the strong, and only the strong, to aim for.

CHAPTER SIX

INDUCEMENT OPERATIONS

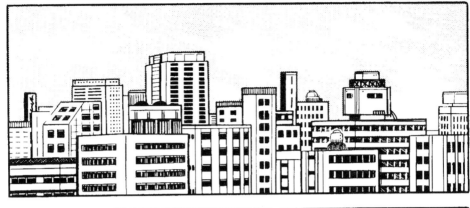

OH! WHAT'S THIS!?

WHAT'S WRONG, RUMIKO?

MR. SAKAMOTO:

I'VE NEVER MET YOU, AND I WON'T BOTHER TO INTRODUCE MYSELF. I'VE ALWAYS HAD AN EASY LIFE. EVEN AFTER I JOINED COMPANY B, THE TOP-RANKING MANUFACTURER IN ITS FIELD, I ADVANCED RAPIDLY, AND WAS ABOUT TO BE PROMOTED TO MANAGER. I DESERVED THE PROMOTION.

THEN I LOST TO YOU IN BATTLE. I TASTED THE BITTERNESS OF DEFEAT FOR THE FIRST TIME EVER. BUT I'M ASKING FOR A REMATCH, AND THIS TIME I WON'T LOSE. I KNOW YOU'RE GOING TO THINK I'M BEING MELODRAMATIC, BUT JUST THINK OF THIS LETTER AS A GRACIOUS WARNING FROM ONE WARRIOR TO ANOTHER.

SHIMADA

THIS *GIVES* ME THE CREEPS ...

137

MEANWHILE, AT COMPANY B ....

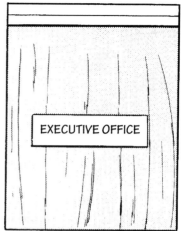

EXECUTIVE OFFICE

OK, OK. IF YOU WANT IT THAT BADLY, I'LL GO ALONG WITH YOU.

WE DON'T KNOW WHAT ELSE TO DO TO GET BACK AT COMPANY W, ANYWAY.

THANK YOU, SIR!

IT'S HARD TO SAY NO TO YOU, SHIMADA.

OPERATION FOX? I LIKE THE NAME. I'LL HELP YOU ALL I CAN.

I PROMISE TO MAKE THIS A SUCCESS.

THE IDEA FOR OPERATION FOX CAME FROM GENERAL ERWIN ROMMEL, WHO COMMANDED GERMANY'S AFRIKA KORPS DURING WORLD WAR II.
THE ALLIES FEARED HIM AND CALLED HIM THE DESERT FOX.

COMPANY B'S BEST AND BRIGHTEST FROM ALL OVER JAPAN GATHER AT THE HEAD OFFICE. PREPARATIONS FOR OPERATION FOX BEGIN.

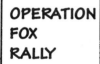

OPERATION FOX RALLY

THIS WILL BE OUR LAST BRIEFING. NOW, A FEW WORDS FROM THE EXECUTIVE DIRECTOR.

YOU ALL KNOW HOW MUCH I'M COUNTING ON YOU.

143

OUR COMPANY IS PLANNING A HUGE CAMPAIGN.

YOU ARE?

WE'RE PLANNING TO CALL ON OUR USERS.

WE'VE RECEIVED ORDERS FROM THE OKUBO AND IKEZAWA COMPANIES. COULD YOU TAKE CARE OF THEM?

SURE! THANKS!

LET'S SEE ... YOUR MONTHLY AVERAGE IS SOMETHING LIKE ...

IF YOU PARTICIPATE IN THIS CAMPAIGN, YOU SHOULD BE ABLE TO IMPROVE ON THAT, JUDGING FROM THE NUMBER OF USERS IN THIS AREA.

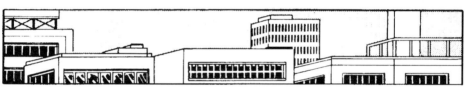

145

YES. WE'VE ALWAYS FEATURED YOUR PRODUCTS. IF WE CAN COUNT ON THIS MUCH ...

NO, YOU SHOULD BE ABLE TO DO BETTER THAN THAT ...

WE'LL BE BACKING YOU UP ALL THE WAY.

WELL, IN THAT CASE ...

THANK YOU VERY MUCH. WE'LL BE COUNTING ON YOU.

THREE WEEKS HAVE PASSED SINCE I GOT THAT "CHALLENGE" LETTER. NOTHING HAS HAPPENED, THOUGH. PSYCHOLOGICAL WARFARE?

CHIEF, MR. KONDO'S TEAM IS IN BIG TROUBLE.

WHAT DO YOU MEAN?

I'M NOT SURE, BUT THE MOOD IS PRETTY TENSE OVER THERE.

147

WONDER IF SHIMADA'S INVOLVED ...

SEEMS TO BE. ANYWAY, THIS REPORT WILL TELL YOU WHAT'S GOING ON.

I'VE BEEN TALKING WITH THE DIRECTOR. WE'VE DECIDED TO PROVIDE COMPANY-WIDE SUPPORT FOR KONDO.

SINCE YOU'RE THE ONE WHO RECEIVED THE CHALLENGE, LET ME KNOW IF YOU NEED HELP.

I WILL. THANK YOU.

SO, SHIMADA'S MADE A MOVE ...

COMPANY W'S COUNTER-ATTACK BEGINS, BUT ...

SORRY, BUT WE JUST CAN'T HANDLE ANY MORE INVENTORY.

OUR WAREHOUSE IS FULL. WE JUST DON'T HAVE ANY ROOM.

COMPANY W'S PLOT IS FOILED. COMPANY B HAS BEATEN THEM TO THE DRAW.

COMPANY B, RIDING HIGH, THEN LAUNCHES A SURPRISE ATTACK ON TAKAOKA'S (COMPANY W) TERRITORY.

ONCE AGAIN, COMPANY W IS PUT ON THE DEFENSIVE.

151

THIS MIGHT BE A *GOOD* TIME TO OFFER BIG DISCOUNTS.

NO, ONCE WE DISCOUNT, THERE'S NO TURNING BACK.

DISCOUNTS WOULD BE SUICIDE.

THEN, WHAT ARE WE GOING TO DO?

....

WE HELD A MANAGERS' MEETING TODAY, WHICH SAKAMOTO ATTENDED.

SAKAMOTO, WHAT ABOUT THE LANCHESTER STRATEGY? DOES IT COVER A SITUATION LIKE THIS?

ACCORDING TO THE STRATEGY OF THE STRONG, WE NEED TO SET UP AN INFORMATION NETWORK IMMEDIATELY TO PREPARE FOR A MATCHING OPERATION.

THAT MAKES SENSE. IN THIS CASE, THE INFORMATION CAME IN MUCH TOO LATE.

WE CAN RESPOND IMMEDIATELY IF WE KNOW WHAT COMPANY B IS UP TO.

WELL, IF THAT'S THE ONLY IDEA, THEN LET'S GET TO WORK. SET UP AN INFORMATION NETWORK RIGHT AWAY.

LOYAL USERS OF COMPANY W'S PRODUCTS AGREE TO CONTACT THE COMPANY WHENEVER THEY SPOT COMPANY B'S GAUDY VEHICLES.

DIRECTOR'S OFFICE

RING
RING
RING

HELLO. YES ... REALLY? THANK YOU VERY MUCH.

SOMEONE SPOTTED COMPANY B'S OPERATION FOX TEAM IN DISTRICT X.

OK, I'LL GET RIGHT ON IT.

HELLO, THIS IS MASUMURA. GO TO DISTRICT X RIGHT AWAY!

155

156

HUH? DISTRICT Z?! YOU'VE GOT TO BE KIDDING!

WHAT'S GOING ON?

... SO THAT'S THE STORY.

I'LL BET THEY'RE USING THE SAME STRATEGY THE AMERICANS DID IN WORLD WAR II.

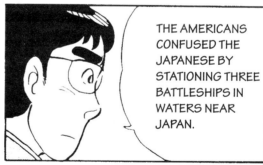

THE AMERICANS CONFUSED THE JAPANESE BY STATIONING THREE BATTLESHIPS IN WATERS NEAR JAPAN.

HMM ... I SEE.

157

PLEASE WAIT A LITTLE LONGER. I HAVE A PLAN.

I HOPE SO. IN FACT, YOU'RE MY ONLY HOPE.

....

OK, MORI. THANKS A LOT.

NOW I KNOW WHAT SHIMADA'S UP TO ... I THINK.

NOW, WHAT DO I DO ABOUT IT?

159

INDUCEMENT OPERATIONS

AN INDUCEMENT OPERATION COUNTERACTS A WEAKER OPPONENT'S DIVERSIONARY OPERATION.

THE STRONG MUST MAKE THE FIRST MOVE SO THAT THE WEAK CAN'T USE THE STRATEGY OF THE WEAK.

IF THE STRONGER OPPONENT GETS TOO FAR AHEAD, THE WEAK CAN'T MAKE A MOVE.

CHECK-MATE

WHEN YOU MAKE THE FIRST MOVE, YOU INDUCE THE WEAK TO IMITATE YOU.

TRY AND FOLLOW THIS.

YOU STYMIE WEAKER RIVALS' ATTEMPTS AT DIFFERENTIATION OR ONE-POINT CONCENTRATION. THAT'S AN INDUCEMENT OPERATION.

BUT YOU'VE GOT TO KNOW WHAT THE ENEMY'S UP TO.

WE'VE BEEN USING MATCHING OPERATIONS — WAITING FOR SHIMADA TO MAKE A MOVE.

I THOUGHT MATCHING OPERATIONS WERE ONE OF THE STRATEGIES OF THE STRONG.

THAT'S TRUE. THEY ARE, BUT ...

BY THE TIME WE CAUGHT ON, SHIMADA WAS ALREADY MAKING HEADWAY WITH OPERATION FOX. WE LET HIM GET AHEAD OF US.

OK, WE'VE GOT TO MAKE THE FIRST MOVE, BUT DO YOU KNOW WHAT HE'S UP TO?

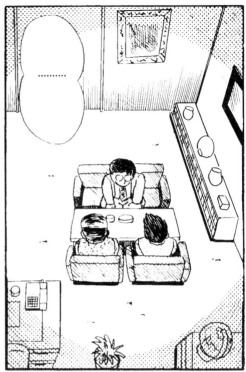

....

I CAN'T GIVE YOU ANY GUARANTEES, BUT ...

TWO DAYS LATER ...

UNDER SHIMADA'S COMMAND, COMPANY B'S ELITE TROOPS LAUNCH A SURPRISE ATTACK ON DISTRICT X.

A USER'S OFFICE ...

I'M SHIMIZU FROM COMPANY B. IS MR. ARAI IN?

I'M SORRY, HE'S ATTENDING A SEMINAR FOR COMPANY W'S USERS.

WHAT ARE YOU DOING HERE?

LOOKS LIKE YOU BEAT ME TO IT.

164

CONFERENCE ROOM

THIS HAS BEEN THE LONGEST MONTH IN OUR COMPANY'S HISTORY. BUT THANKS TO ALL OF YOU, WE WON OUR BATTLE WITH COMPANY B.

ACCORDING TO THE LANCHESTER STRATEGY, WE'RE NUMBER ONE NOW.

BEING NUMBER ONE MEANS THAT YOU'RE IN SUCH A STRONG POSITION THAT YOU CAN'T BE REVERSED.

BUT A RIVAL COULD COME INTO SHOOTING RANGE AT ANY TIME. KEEP ALERT!

166

TO MAKE OUR NUMBER-ONE POSITION ABSOLUTELY IMPENETRABLE, I'VE DECIDED TO OPEN SOME BRANCH OFFICES NEXT MONTH.

WE'LL BE INCREASING THE NUMBER OF OUR BASES.

AND WE'LL BE JOINING THE LANCHESTER STRATEGY RESEARCH GROUP.

THE PRESIDENT HAS AGREED TO ESTABLISH AN EDUCATION PROGRAM. IF ANYONE WANTS TO SIGN UP FOR A LANCHESTER SEMINAR, LET ME KNOW.

GOOD WORK, MORI! DISTRICT X WILL BE A CHALLENGE, BUT GIVE IT YOUR BEST.

I CAN'T BELIEVE THEY GAVE THIS JOB TO A YOUNG GUY LIKE ME. I'M NERVOUS.

YOU'LL BE FINE. IT'S A CONSERVATIVE AREA, SO YOU MAY HAVE TROUBLE AT FIRST. BUT I HAVE FAITH IN YOU.

I'LL BE RELYING ON WHAT YOU TAUGHT ME ABOUT THE NEW LANCHESTER STRATEGY.

THAT'S THE SPIRIT!

EXCUSE ME FOR INTERRUPTING YOU.

MR. KONDO...

UH ... WELL, I, UH ...

THANKS, SAKAMOTO!

I DIDN'T KNOW THAT YOUR ADVICE HELPED OUR TEAM BECOME NUMBER ONE.

I JUST HEARD THAT FROM YOKOYAMA.

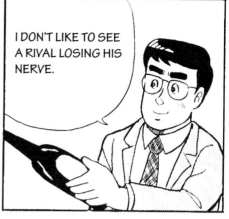

I DON'T LIKE TO SEE A RIVAL LOSING HIS NERVE.

HA, HA ... I GUESS I DESERVED THAT.

I'VE ALWAYS GIVEN YOU A HARD TIME, I KNOW ...

BUT I'M GOING TO START STUDYING THE LANCHESTER STRATEGY IN EARNEST.

BUT TELL ME, HOW DID YOU GET ONTO SHIMADA'S PLAN?

THAT'S EASY. I GOT MORI TO CHECK UP ON HIM.

I FOUND OUT THAT HIS HOBBY IS OTHELLO, THE GAME.

RIGHT. THEN I PLOTTED THE TERRITORIES HE'D ATTACKED ON THIS MAP.

OTHELLO? THE ONE WITH THE BLACK AND WHITE PIECES?

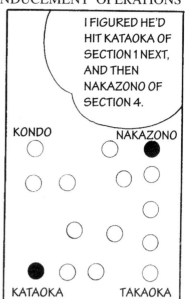

NOW IT MAKES SENSE! IN OTHELLO, IF YOU CAPTURE A CORNER, YOU'VE WON, RIGHT?

YOU KNOW, HIS "CHALLENGE LETTER" TO US WAS A DIVERSIONARY OPERATION.

IT HELPED THAT HE'S GOT A LOT OF PRIDE.

HE WAS SO SHOCKED WHEN WE FIGURED OUT WHAT HE WAS DOING THAT HE JUST GAVE UP.

BUT HE'S REALLY SHARP. IT'S A GOOD THING WE DIDN'T MAKE ANY MISTAKES.

IMAGINE MODELLING YOUR SALES STRATEGY ON A GAME!

174

WHEN PEOPLE GET OBSESSED, THEIR TRUE NATURES COME OUT. ESPECIALLY WHEN THEY'RE AS METICULOUS AS SHIMADA.

WE DON'T HAVE TO WORRY ABOUT THAT.

LOOK! IT'S THE CHIEF AND MR. KONDO!

THEY'LL ALWAYS BE RIVALS, BUT IT'LL BE A HEALTHIER RIVALRY.

ANYWAY, WE'RE ALL RIVALS, AREN'T WE.

SUMMARY

When you engage in an inducement operation, you are luring your enemy into a situation where you have the upper hand.

The weak will engage in decoy or feint operations that prevent the strong from determining the former's real objective. The strong should consider making the first move, distracting the weak, and preventing them from launching such offensives.

In ancient times, armies made use of inducement operations. They would chase the enemy into a valley or an impasse, and then throw rocks or boiling water down upon its forces. More recently, tactics like spreading rumors that a particular unit of yours is weak, and then launching an all-out attack when the enemy swallows the bait and attacks, have been used.

The stronger army can be virtually assured of victory, if it can manage to discover the enemy's plans and to induce the enemy to play into its hands.

In sales strategy, too, strong companies should launch inducement operations. The basic strategy for the strong is the matching strategy, but if matching operations continue to be forestalled, the weaker enemy picks up strength. In cases like this, the strong need to make the first move, thus preventing the weak from using the strategy of the weak.

Japanese companies often react emotionally, meaning that they tend to retaliate against a rival that has gotten ahead of them by imitating the rival's moves. This is connected to the idea of the stronger company's getting the jump on its weaker rival and forcing that rival to imitate it (not allowing it to differentiate).

Manufacturers would do well to develop many new products, thus getting ahead of their weaker rivals. Even when it seems that those weaker rivals have outdone them, the strong, when they get hold of advance information suggesting that a weaker rival is about to develop a new product, should manufacture copycat products, and get them on the market ahead of the rival. If they succeed in doing that, the weak will have to reconsider the wisdom of introducing their new product, because since they're late, no one will notice it.

177

When the strong cannot forestall the weaker rival's new product appearance, they should pursue the matching option. Remember, though, that getting your product on the market as soon as possible after your rival does will help to lessen the impact of the rival product.

The matching operation assumes speed. When you cannot launch a matching operation, i.e., get your product on the market, as soon as you would like to, be sure to issue advance publicity or advertising at the earliest possible moment. This will prompt customers to think, "Well, if Company X is going to come out with a similar product, perhaps I'll wait." Then your weaker rival will have an uphill battle with its new product.

Wholesalers should snap up new products that their competitors are hesitating over. They must keep abreast of advancements, such as new types of media (business systems, for instance). The strong have access to much more information than do the weak. Furthermore, they have the time, energy, and financial resources to get ahead of the competition.

Retailers and services should divest themselves of traditional biases and prejudices, and be quick to incorporate techniques that have brought other industries success.

As far as regional strategy is concerned, if the strong can find out which regions the weak have targeted in advance, they can make the first move and focus on those regions. If that isn't possible, they can themselves target regions where the weak are likely to launch a concentrated attack of the local-battle type. In that case, the weak will be forced to expend energy on a wide-area-battle-type market, where they are clearly at a disadvantage.

If all else fails, and you, the strong company, are faced with a regional attack, then match that attack promptly. By doing so, you will have diluted the impact of the weak's one-point concentration efforts.

To launch an inducement operation, you first need to know what your enemy is up to. Once you have that information, the rest should be easy. If you can continue to stay one step ahead of the weaker competition, your position should remain secure. Your first priority is to acquire as much information as possible. That capability will permit you to defend yourself successfully.

178

FAX ORDER FORMS TO: 408-732-7723
LANCHESTER PRESS INC.
P.O. BOX 60621 SUNNYVALE, CA 94086

Name_____ Tel._____

Company_____ Fax._____

Addr._____

_____

_____

City._____ State.____Zip._____

Payment Information:

VISA [   ]   MC [   ]   Check [   ]   Money Order [   ]

Cardholder └┴┴┴┴┴┴┴┴┴┴┴┴┴┴┴┴┴┴┴┴┴┴┘

Number. └┴┴┴┴┘ - └┴┴┴┴┘ - └┴┴┴┴┘ - └┴┴┴┘

Signature._____